RUPTURE

RUPTURE

POEMS

ADRIE ROSE

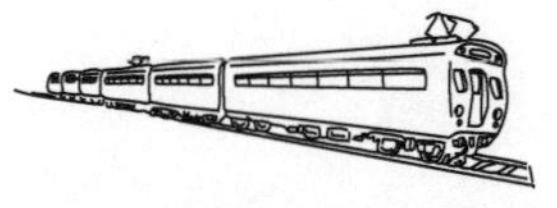

Gold Line Press

Cover and book design by David Wojciechowski
Cover art by Wyxina Tresse, Unsplash

Published by Gold Line Press
http://goldlinepress.com

Gold Line Press titles are distributed by Small Press Distribution
This title is also available for purchase directly from the publisher
www.spdbooks.org / 800-869-7553

Library of Congress Cataloging-in-Publication Data

Rupture / Adrie Rose

Library of Congress Control Number 2023943451
Rose, Adrie
ISBN: 978-1-938900-50-1

"Depression is rage internalized," my second therapist told
me. I had squelched and winnowed and edited my rage
down to something that looked like sadness. Something
that didn't shimmer like anger, but glistened with a dull, flat
endlessness. I had stuck my burning so deep that I couldn't
feel it, not for years. I had to go down into the dark of me,
where I'd shoved rage, and call her back up.

—*Marissa Korbel*

I for my part will go down singing,
have come thus far…

—*Kevin Goodan*

to Jojo and Susu —
you carry my heart in your hearts

Table of Contents

Rupture

I.

Later there will be a bill
in dollars
and cents,
but here
in the operating room
we barter —

I give them
a pint
of blood,

flesh that might
have been a baby,

one fallopian tube
and they give me

three scars and
my life.

II.

5 a.m. I wake
and can't return
to sleep — stomach
throbbing, hospital band still
clamped on my wrist.

The rain lets loose her hair
outside. He
is asleep
in my bed.
His body. Un-
marked.

III.

That first
morning, there is
blood — expected
— but the musk

of after
birth
I am not
prepared for.

I understand,
suddenly,
that a baby
has died,

caught in the tangle
of my body, gone
before we knew
it was there.

I am clotted
in the iron dark
smell. Someone
is weeping.

Hunted Season

Before that — we walked naked to the edge, meadow kissing forest. Both of us found spots to pee after making love. Behind me, the startled *whumph* of a large animal snorting. *Bear*, I thought, and right away you said, *It's not a bear*, but waved me back anyway into the silvered meadow. *It's a stag*.

We listened as he pawed the ground behind the darkened trees and snuffled, moved away on his unseen trail. Inside me, the egg snagged, began silently to fissure. You stood between me and the stag. Each of us certain we knew who to fear.

Before

kissing

you

listen
behind the dark

between me and the
stag,
fear.

The Cello

As if I had only heard music through a fuzzy radio,
and suddenly found myself in the middle of the orchestra

with the timpani vibrating up through my feet, and above all
the piccolo soaring toward its peak. I felt every small

movement. I knew how the unbroken pond feels when the stone
enters, the undulation of each ripple towards shore. For days,

when I thought of you, my hand went to my throat,
my body vibrating, like the cello when the soloist

has set down her bow — polished with sweat,
the strings still humming, see how even the air

around them shimmers.

The Nurse Calls After the Ectopic Pregnancy

After your own body is the bomb.
The honest diagnosis:
you will be too weak to lift
a jug of milk. If you stay up
past ten, you will fever
and headache for days.
You will need a sweater
even though it is August.

You will fear that you never
went to the ER and that you
are actually dead now.

We will clear you
to go back to work after
two weeks, but
you should not go back
for two months. Or
maybe two years.
We have saved what life
you have. There are no refills.

                I'm lying.
                She only
                handed me
                a prescription
                for birth control pills
                as they wheeled
                me out.

The Bell

I wanted to know
what it was like to receive
without hesitation
and so
I was the mortar
and you the pestle,
I was the pool
and you the waterfall,
I was the bell and you
the tongue,
until
I was not
myself,
only
       the humming,
            only the golden,
                 being rung
                     and rung and rung.

I Don't Want Any More Babies, And Yet

Each month
     frayed, like a blooming

fruit tree after
     a night of heavy rains.

The lining
     dissolves, the body

gives up
     another not

born,
     this ordinary

grief,
     all

        that has   not   become.

Spring—& Everyone Seems So Fucking Happy

No seeds to sow.
The taste
of silt. Scorched grass.
My rage?
There is no time,
no cradle for it.
This morning, shaky again,
I drop the spoon, flip
over the bowl of oatmeal
as I try to stir it cool.

Once my living children
are tucked
into school, I return
to the frost forest,
the banks above the ice river
where despair can slip
along, carving
the rocks, sending
moss as messenger
for all that was taken.

*I walked where we harvested
wild blueberries*, he writes.
The ghost and I
do not write back.

I want my body
before it knew his
body. I gather and weave
what protections
I can — yarrow, knot-
weed, wild rose.

With no harbor
for anger, exhaustion
pulls me down
in its net.

The sheets
are a shroud
and I will sew them closed
with my breath.

I trust no one, especially
not myself anymore. I ask
the land — *Bones
of the Mother
I have loved,
open to me.*

There is a holler

where the deer sleep
beneath the elderberries.
I lay there, back of my heart

to the soil. In a dream,
grandmother said, "You won't
get this chance much, honey,
so cry now," and took me
into her arms, onto her lap,
and I wept.

Under the elder,
yarrow grows —
leaves that show
where they were cut
right to the bones.
The lucky ones.

Radiant

Here
  there is no endpoint,
    no destination, here is radiant

touch, now
  urgent, the rolling
    circling of us

here but also in
  worlds unseen, my song
    trumpets through you and yours

through me, we are
  quickened, let
    us enter

completely, let us
              be undone.

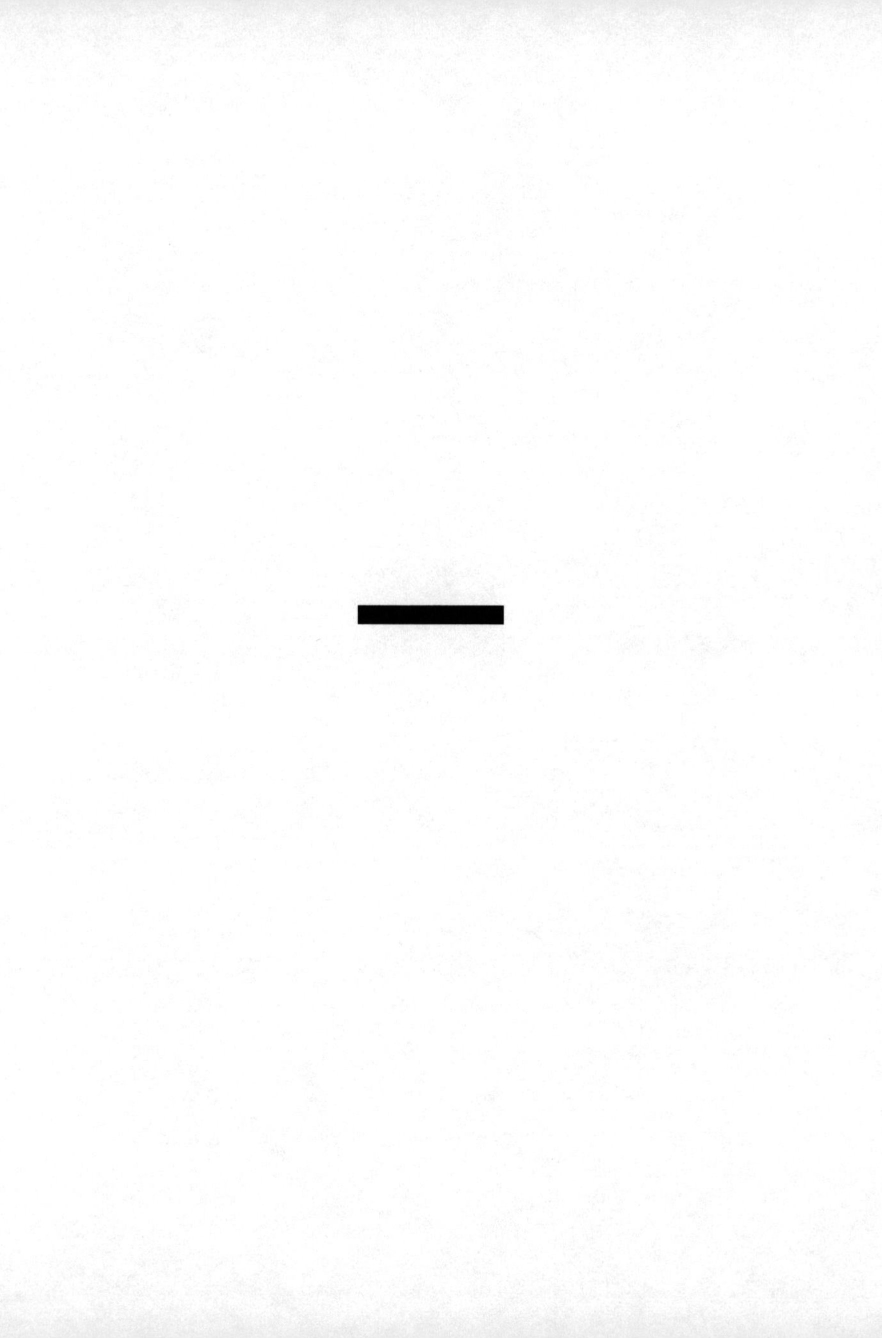

In July, Weeds Take Over the Garden

I am no expert at saving things.
Sweaters eaten
by moths, teeth
lost, artwork haphazardly
recycled or kept.

Who chooses
what survives, and why?
July brings back roses

everywhere as if
we were celebrating.
The baby would be born now.
When I dropped

the jar of dried calendula,
glass shards leapt
into every corner of the room.
Even after

I swept, they surfaced
and pierced us.
Even years later.

Unexpected Again

I.

August, unwanted month,
kept returning.
Geese honked, barking
us away from their goslings.

We saw lily pads far out
on the water, and he said,
Let's go see them, I'll
take you.

He paddled the small canoe
closer to the lilies —
golden, surprisingly stiff
when I touched them.

The wind blew.
He paddled us to shore again.
He did not turn once
to look back
and see me.

II.

I find,
unexpected again,
that the bills still demand
to be paid, the children
to be fed, even this body
asks, finally, to eat,

to sleep, even pursued
by unwanted dreams.

The heart
insists
everything
has stopped.

The bones
keep walking.

III.

There will be surprises.

Your lover — who came to the ER
hours late, reeking of pot,
who left the day after and never
fully returned —
will read your journal
and take all of his belongings
from your house.
His pillow from the bed, his sage
from the altar.

There are
roses. The wind
on the harbor.
Alone at a cafe, you write:
>   *At last,*
>   *I miss no one.*

It's True I Liked Our Blazing

That first night, I
woke to him kissing me.

No, he said, laughing, *I woke
to* you *kissing* me.

That first night, we
       we woke up kissing,
dreams a quilt
       we pulled up
and down, woke
       again. Kissing.

We

       up

  woke —

       kissing   sleep
                       then —

          and

              again

Near Solstice

Cocoon of deep snow,
        sleep and not-sleep by the fire.

I walk the mountain
        where we planned a wedding,

lay down footsteps over
        footsteps, seal and bind the past

so it stays past. Now the baby would be
        six months old. Now nine months.

The nurses brought saltines
        and ginger ale, warned about cramping,

tenderly held my clenched
        hand. He posts photos of himself with

his new lover, his face turned away. I press
        to see if I am still bruised, wake

in the night to load the stove
        so the pipes don't freeze.

Listen to the house crack and shriek
        as the cold wrenches wood from nails.

If spring comes, I will plant
        peach trees.

Will spread wood ash
          to sweeten the soil.

Will greet violets like friends
          returning, like the only gifts left

to me — purple lobes
          shining darkly in the grass.

I wake and feed
          the fire, sleep and do not sleep.

The temperature keeps falling
          around me. I stay.

Throat of the Blossom

Before the swelling buds,
        the thrusting leaves of crocus,
                there is the fruitless

winter, empty sheets
        of snow upon snow.
                What wants to come through,

will. Here
        is a woman
                putting on a dress

for no lover
        but the first heats
                of spring.

Who knows
        what happens next —
                the fallow field touched

by wind, the throat
        of the blossom brushed
                by the pollen heavy bee.

The Knife, Sharpened

         I   sold
the diamond ring, swept
the corners of the rooms, slept
with a pine branch
beside me.

         How   long
it has taken to find every stray
clipping to throw into the fire.

The wolf in the bed
said, *You owe me,*
you opened
your door.

         How   long
does it take, yarrow
on the doorstep,
wedding dress
given away,
a pint   of blood
taken, all bribes

returned,
all debts   paid.

Notes

The Marissa Korbel epigraph is from her essay in *Guernica*, "Why We Cry When We're Angry."

The Kevin Goodan epigraph is from "Almanac of Caliber and Distance" in *In The Ghost-House Acquainted*.

Yarrow is a wild plant found around the globe, which has a long history of medicinal and magical use in many traditions. The stems were used for divination with the I Ching, and are used for magical help with boundaries and protection. Medicinally, it has many uses, and is most known for its ability to quickly stop bleeding when applied externally to a wound, and to promote healing of even deep cuts and wounds. The leaves of the plant are feathered, and herbalist Matthew Wood notes that we can apply the doctrine of signatures to them–the leaves look as though they were cut back to the bone (stem) of the plant. These qualities are referenced throughout this collection, as yarrow was (and remains) an important plant ally to me.

Ectopic pregnancies refer to a pregnancy where a fertilized egg doesn't implant in the lining of the uterus, but instead implants elsewhere, usually in the fallopian tube, and begins to grow there. This results in internal bleeding, which can lead to death of the pregnant person, if it isn't found and treated soon enough. If caught very early, medications can be used, but usually there needs to be surgical removal of the egg and the split fallopian tube, and sometimes even the uterus. The pregnancy is not viable. Early symptoms include spotting and pelvic pain, increasing to severe abdominal pain, shoulder pain, and lightheadedness or fainting. One in fifty pregnancies in the US is ectopic. After having one ectopic pregnancy, chances increase of having another.

"Radiant" was previously published in *PoetryBreakfast.com*.

"The Cello," "Rupture," "It's True I Liked Our Blazing," and "The Nurse Calls After the Ectopic Pregnancy" were previously published in *Emulate*.

"In July, Weeds Take Over the Garden" was previously published in *Muzzle*.

"The Knife, Sharpened" was previously published in *The Night Heron Barks*.

"Rupture" was published in the 2022 Anhinga Press anthology *Rumors, Secrets, & Lies: poems about pregnancy, abortion & choice*.

"Near Solstice" and "There is a holler," were previously published in the 2022 Porkbelly Press anthology *haunted*.

Gratitudes

With so much gratitude to Joseph and Susan, whose love continues to carry me through. With love and thanks to Jen, Cailin, and Chris, for friendship and Sunday morning parents' call. To Jody, first reader and auntie and cheerleader extraordinaire. To Tiana Clark, whose wisdom and guidance brought so much to these pages, and to the capstone class, who asked about the speaker's anger. To Ellen Doré Watson, for many wonderful poetry classes. To Hugo, who liked to sleep by my heart. To my parents and children, for putting up with my everyday nonsense. To Sarah, who was there and was my friend. To the Ada Comstock program at Smith College, for giving me the chance to return to school and to poetry. Gratitude to Bryan and Sara and Gold Line Press for the incredible opportunity and support bringing these words out into the world. With tremendous thanks to Courtney Faye Taylor, for choosing this collection. To Tim, my most romatic friend, who I get to grow with.

Adrie Rose lives next to an orchard in Western MA and is the editor of Nine Syllables Press at Smith College. She is a Poetry MFA student at Warren Wilson College. Her work has previously appeared in *The Baltimore Review*, *Nimrod*, *The Night Heron Barks*, *Underblong*, the *Ploughshares* blog, and more. She won the Elizabeth Babcock Poetry Prize, the Ethel Olin Corbin Prize, and the Gertrude Posner Spencer Prize in 2021, and the Anne Bradstreet Prize, the Eleanor Cederstrom Prize, and the Mary Augusta Jordan Prize in 2022. Find her on Instagram @AdrieRose_

PGIL2023USA